CW00957225

MOULE'S COUNTY MAPS

THE WEST
OF ENGLAND

ENGLANDS

TOPOGRAPHER

or

W R

MOULE'S ENGLISH COUNTIES

IN THE 19th. CENTURY.

By

THOMAS MOULE,

Author of Bibliotheca, Heraldica & Editor of several popular Topographical Works.

London,

Geo. Virtue, 26, Ivy Lane, Simpkin & Marshall, Stationers Court,

1836.

MOULE'S COUNTY MAPS

THE WEST
OF ENGLAND

INCLUDING
THE WEST MIDLANDS

THOMAS MOULE

Introduced by
Ashley Baynton-Williams

BRACKEN BOOKS
LONDON

PUBLISHER'S NOTE

The local descriptions accompanying the plates in this book have been
compiled from a variety of Victorian sources which
are listed in the Bibliography on page 48.

This edition published 1994 by Bracken Books, an imprint of Studio
Editions Ltd., Princess House, 50 Eastcastle Street,
London W1N 7AP, England.

Copyright © 1994 Studio Editions Ltd.

All rights reserved. No part of this publication may be reproduced,
stored in a retrieval system, or transmitted, in any form or by any
means, electronic, mechanical, photocopying, recording or otherwise,
without the prior permission in writing of the copyright holder.

ISBN 1 85891 196 6

Copy-edited by Christine O'Brien
Designed by Peter Champion and Paul Effeny

Printed and bound by Poligrafici Calderara S.p.a., Bologna, Italy

Frontispiece, Decorative title-page and verso from The English Counties
Delineated *by Thomas Moule, 1837.*

CONTENTS

England and Wales *from* The English Counties Delineated *by Thomas Moule, 1837.*
Coloured boundary lines clearly delineate the 52 counties of nineteenth-century England and Wales.

INTRODUCTION

Accustomed as the modern map-user is to the Ordnance Survey maps of the British Isles, we should nevertheless remember that they represent a relatively recent development in the cartographic history of these islands. When the Ordnance Survey was first undertaken in 1791, England already had a well-established tradition of regional map-making going back, in printed form, for 200 years. In contrast to the Ordnance Survey, the majority of these maps were constructed on a county-by-county basis, with over 100 different series of county atlases being published between 1579 and 1900.

During the last 80 years, as many of the traditional counties have been effaced from the map, there has been an increasing interest in old maps that focus on each of the 52 counties that made up eighteenth-century England and Wales. Although every one of the different series has an individual claim to fame, among the most popular are the maps from Moule's *The English Counties Delineated*, published in 1837.

MOULE'S COUNTY MAPS

Thomas Moule (1784–1851) was inspector of 'blind letters' (ones with illegible addresses) for the Post Office, but he was also a one-time bookseller, an author on English and Continental architecture and a contributor to William Westall's *Great Britain Illustrated*. A man of varied interests, Moule was also the author of works on heraldry and genealogy. With this varied background, it is hardly surprising that he conceived an ambitious plan to publish an atlas of England and Wales.

On account of the scale of this undertaking, Moule chose to issue the atlas in parts, or more properly monthly numbers. This was a common practice at the time, since it allowed publishers to recoup their costs as they went along and spread the payments for would-be purchasers. (Indeed, some of Dickens' novels were issued in this fashion.) The monthly numbers were issued between 1830 and 1837, each with a map and a section of descriptive text relating to the county, written by Moule himself. In the Preface, Moule claimed to have visited every county of England, except Derbyshire and Cornwall, when compiling the text. In 1837, when the series was complete, the parts were bound together, and issued as *The English Counties Delineated*. In addition to the county maps, there were maps of the Isles of Wight, Man and Thanet, the environs of London, Bath and Bristol, Plymouth and Devonport and Portsmouth, a four-sheet map of the 'Inland Navigation', and plans of London, Bath, Boston in Lincolnshire, Oxford and Cambridge.

Moule's maps are celebrated as the last series of county maps to blend together both geographical and decorative features in their visual design so as to reflect the author's varied and fascinating interests. It seems as though every inch of the engraved area is utilized to full advantage, containing as it does the map itself, views of principal buildings, coats of arms and elaborate architectural borders. This happy and judicious blend helps to explain the popularity this series has enjoyed both in its own day and among modern admirers and collectors. Then, as now, the maps speak of a rural paradise, of seamless continuity with the past, of prosperity, but above all of a sense of calm and stability.

Yet these very maps were issued in perhaps the most turbulent period in modern British history, as revolutionary change, and even revolution, beckoned. However much Moule's work seems to stand apart from this change, the enormous success that his atlas achieved was made possible by the technological advances associated with the Industrial Revolution. While the roots of the Industrial Revolution lay in the eighteenth century, it was the first half of the nineteenth century that saw scientific discoveries transformed into tangible realities, as understanding turned into application; and these innovations brought considerable benefits to map-making and publishing.

At the beginning of the nineteenth century, printing plates were made from thin sheets of copper, onto which the image would be engraved. This was an intaglio process, which means that the picture was cut into the plate by use of an engraving tool or acid. When printing, the plate would be inked and then wiped with a cloth so as to remove the ink from the highly-polished surface but leaving it in the engraved grooves in the plate. The paper would then be placed over the plate in a press, which

Hereford *from* The British
Atlas: Comprising a Complete
Set of County Maps of
England and Wales *by G. Cole
and J. Roper, c. 1801. A medieval city, Hereford gave its name
to its county, Herefordshire. Once
capital of the ancient kingdom of
Mercia, ruled by the celebrated
King Otta, Hereford today retains
much of its original charm.*

forced the two together and transferred the ink onto the paper. Copper had been used since 1477, when the first atlas was printed. It had the advantage of being relatively soft, so it could be engraved, and corrected, easily. However, its softness also made it susceptible to wear, particularly as great pressure was exerted during printing, and this could be visible after only a few hundred examples had been printed. Once this happened, the plate would have to be reworked to strengthen the engraved lines: a laborious process. In all, perhaps only 1,000, or at most 2,000 examples could be printed from one copper-plate. The new

technology introduced paper-making machines, which could produce paper faster and more cheaply (though admittedly of a lesser quality) than the hand-made techniques used at the beginning of the century. Earliest versions of the steam-press were able to print four times faster than the old hand-press. The effect was to make printing far less expensive. All that was necessary was a more suitable printing plate.

In the 1820s, publishers started using steel plates instead of copper. Steel had the benefit of being much harder and more durable. A skilled engraver could also produce a finer line on a steel plate, bringing greater detail to the engraving. The main drawback was that steel was more difficult to engrave, and to revise. However, its durability meant that substantially more examples could be printed before the plate deteriorated – Moule claimed that 10,000 sets were subscribed for, although today only one, incomplete, set of the original parts survives.

Perhaps the single greatest catalyst of change was James Watt's invention of the steam-engine, harnessing power for practical use. This discovery not only made possible the factory economy but also led to the introduction and widespread development of the railway network, which linked the factories together and then provided the means of moving factory products to distribution centres and ultimately to their markets, whether in the near vicinity, or in London or indeed in any country in the world.

THE WESTERN REGION

The paradox of the Industrial Revolution is that its dramatic effects fell unevenly. In medieval England, the focal point of the county was the county town; in many cases, the county town gave name to its county – for example, Warwick, Oxford, Worcester, Gloucester and Hereford. These cities were also important, in a predominantly agricultural economy, as centres of distribution.

The Industrial Revolution brought about the transformation of England from a largely peasant-based agrarian economy into an industrial complex, concentrated in the new industrial centres. Improved agricultural machinery increased production but was less labour-intensive. Faced with rural unemployment, people in their thousands left the fields and migrated to urban centres to look for work. For the south-western counties, which did not reap the benefits of industrialization, the result was a substantial decline in population.

One town of early eminence to be passed by was Hereford, a medieval city and capital of the Anglo-Saxon kingdom of Mercia, which retains much of its pre-industrial nature today. For Hereford, however, final judgement was served by the railway companies, when the town was ignored by the planners of the initial rail network. Altogether, the network was much less extensive in the south-west than in the northern counties. The main routes radiated from Bristol – to Birmingham, to London (via the Great Western), to Exeter and from there to Plymouth. This disparity between the industrial north and the largely agricultural south-west became increasingly evident as the nineteenth century wore on.

Hereford, however, was not the only town to be affected by national changes. Just as the county towns of the region failed to benefit, so too did its great port, Bristol. The first sea-port of England in the Middle Ages, Bristol was superseded by Liverpool in the first half of the nineteenth century, partly as a consequence of the latter's better harbour facilities. Liverpool's development to a position of pre-eminence started with the construction of the wet dock, designed in 1709, which used floodgates to overcome the problems of the tide. This, the first of its kind in the world, much expanded the city's dock facilities. Liverpool also proved to be better sited for the trade with America than Bristol, and its proximity to the new industrial regions of the Midlands and North confirmed the new order.

As population shifts occurred, it became clear that the existing parliamentary structure was in need of substantial overhaul. The voting system that existed at the start of the nineteenth century was the result of haphazard and piecemeal evolution over many centuries. The result was a system ruled by anomalies and haunted by corrupt practices. For example, those excluded from voting (and from holding office) were not only children, lunatics and convicted criminals, but also women, Nonconformists, Roman Catholics, Quakers, Jews and agnostics. Moreover, individual boroughs were entitled to exercise their own, additional, rules, to determine eligibility to vote.

It has been estimated that in 1793, when the population stood at 8,500,000 people, 257 of the 513 MPs representing England and Wales were returned by a total of only 11,075 voters; 51 constituencies had under 50 voters, and 130 boroughs had under 300 voters. In particular, the voting system favoured established boroughs and did not take into account population shifts. Thus, Cornwall, which was notorious for its rotten boroughs, paid 16 out of 513 parts of the land-tax, but returned 42 MPs. Lancashire, which paid ten times as much, had 16 MPs. Both Birmingham and Manchester went unrepresented, while the borough of Dunwich, which was half under the sea, had two MPs, one for every seven voters.

In 1832, Parliament acknowledged these failings, and passed the Reform Bill, which established the mechanism for a complete overhaul of the electoral system. The primary step was the complete revision of existing constituencies. Commissioners were appointed to draw up a report, *Municipal Corporation Boundaries (England and Wales)*. This laid down the new constituency boundaries which formed the basis for the modern constituencies of the British Parliament.

As the boundaries were established, Moule incorporated them into his maps (for example, on the Herefordshire map) and noted the numbers of MPs for each county. For Cornwall, there were to be 14, four from the country and ten from the towns.

The charming historical documents collected in this volume provide a fascinating visual record of a bygone time. Although produced with modern technology, the maps retain an antiquarian feel; yet this same modern technology enabled their production in numbers large enough to make them readily available, and affordable, for the modern private collector.

PLATE 1

SHROPSHIRE

Thomas Moule

The English Counties Delineated, 1837

Shropshire is an English county, 44 miles in length and 28 in breadth, which is bounded by Cheshire, Denbighshire, Montgomeryshire, Herefordshire and Staffordshire. It contains 170 parishes and 16 market towns. The principal rivers are the Severn, which runs through the midst of the county, the Terne, the Clun and the Rhea, with several other small streams. The west and south parts are mountainous, some points being nearly 2,000 feet high, and several surpassing 1,000; but the east and north are more plain and level. However, the soil is pretty fertile everywhere, yielding corn and pastures, besides coal, iron and other commodities. The air is sharp on the tops of the hills and mountains, but in the lower parts temperate enough. The great branches of manufacturing industry carried on here are all kinds of ironworks, woollens and china, earthenware and so on. Shropshire has a population of 239,048 and sends 11 members to Parliament.

SHREWSBURY

Shrewsbury, the capital of the county, is so called from the Saxon word Scrobbesberig, which signifies a town built on a woody hill. It is well built, well lighted and well paved, and is the chief market for a coarse kind of woollen cloth made in Montgomeryshire, called Welsh webs, which is bought up in all parts of the country and dressed here. Much of the Welsh flannel is also bought at Welshpool by the drapers of this place, which is indeed a common market for all sorts of Welsh commodities. One great ornament of this town is the Quarry, one of the finest promenades in England. It is beautifully situated in a sort of horseshoe, formed by the river Severn, 154 miles from London. Markets for corn, cattle and provisions are held on Wednesdays and Saturdays; and on Thursdays for Welsh cottons, friezes and flannels. There are fairs on the Saturday after March 15, the Wednesday after Easter week, the Wednesday before Holy Thursday and on July 3, August 12, October 2 and December 12. The population numbers 21,517.

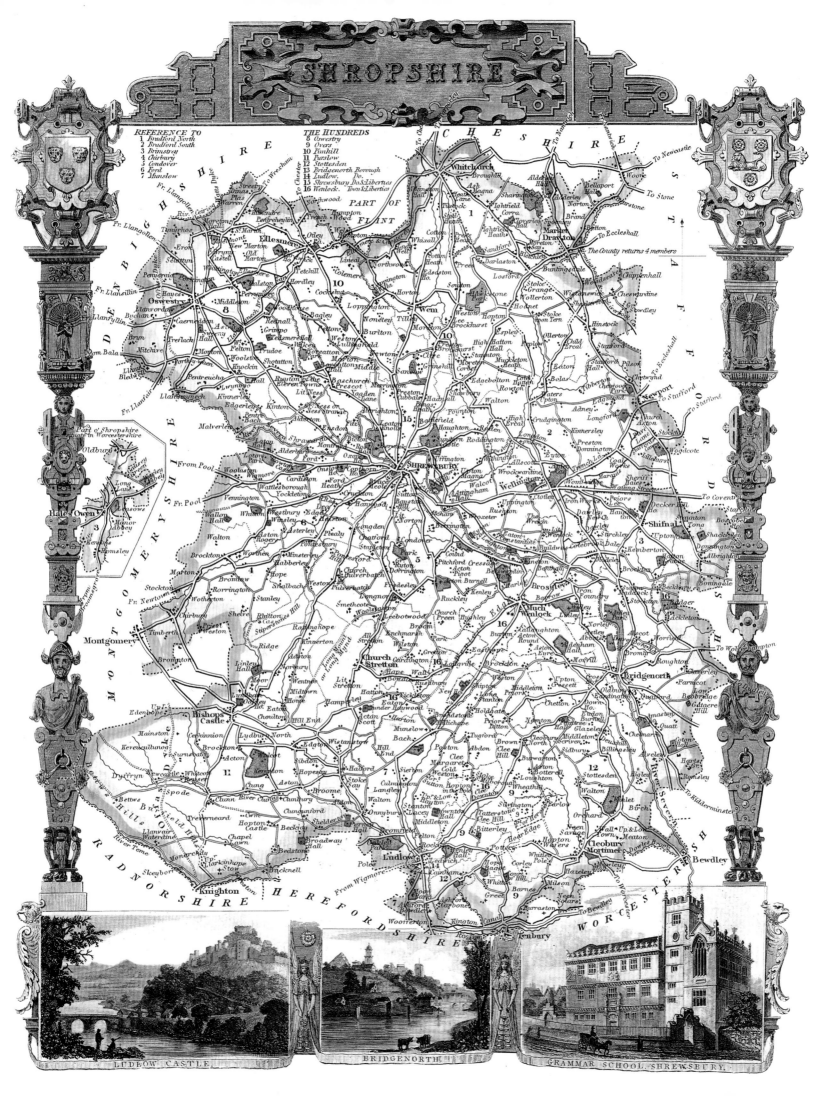

SHROPSHIRE

LUDLOW CASTLE

BRIDGENORTH

GRAMMAR SCHOOL, SHREWSBURY.

PLATE 2

STAFFORDSHIRE

Thomas Moule

The English Counties Delineated, 1837

Staffordshire is a county of England, bounded by Shropshire, Cheshire, Derbyshire, Warwickshire and Worcestershire. It is about 54 miles in length, and varies in breadth from 18 to 36 miles. It contains one city, 21 towns, 181 parishes and 670 villages. The principal rivers are the Trent, Dove, Sow, Churnet, Stour, Penk and Manifold. The air is reckoned pleasant, mild and wholesome. The middle and southern parts are level and plain, and the soil is good and rich; the north is hilly and full of heaths and moors. Staffordshire is famous for its potteries, its inland navigations, and its foundries, blast furnaces, slitting mills and various other branches of the iron trade. The mines of coals, copper, lead and iron ore are rich and extensive; and there are also numerous quarries of stone, alabaster and limestone. The population of Staffordshire is 510,504. The county sends 17 members to Parliament.

STAFFORD

Stafford, the county town, has a free-school and a fine square market-place, in which is a handsome county-hall and under it the market-house. The streets are large, and many of the houses are handsomely built. It manufactures cloth and shoes. The town is situated in a plain on the River Sow, near a navigable canal, 135 miles from London. A market is held on Saturdays. The population is 10,370.

TRENT

A large river, the Trent rises in Staffordshire, issuing from three springs between Congleton and Leek. Flowing through Staffordshire, it enters Derbyshire, crosses the southern angle of that county, and forms for a short space its separation from the counties of Lincoln and Nottingham; it then enters the latter county, and crossing it forms the boundary between that county and Lincolnshire, a corner of which it crosses, and then falls into the Humber below Gainsborough, after a course of about 200 miles, during which it receives the waters of several large streams. It is a large navigable river through the whole of Nottinghamshire, but has the inconvenience of being subject to great and frequent floods.

STAFFORDSHIRE

STAFFORD CASTLE

LICHFIELD CATHEDRAL

REFERENCE
to the
HUNDREDS

1 Cuttleston
2 Offlow
3 Pirehill
4 Seisdon
5 Totmonslow

STAFFORD

The County returns 4 members.

Scale of Miles.
0 1 2 3 4 5 6 7

Railway Stations. thus ●

INGESTRE HOUSE, SEAT OF EARL TALBOT.

PLATE 3

HEREFORDSHIRE

Thomas Moule

The English Counties Delineated, 1837

A county of England lying next to Wales, Herefordshire is bounded by Shropshire, Gloucestershire, Worcestershire and Monmouthshire. It extends about 38 miles from north to south and 33 from east to west. It contains one city, six market towns, 176 parishes and 391 villages. The air is healthy, the climate mild and the soil generally fertile, producing wheat, barley, oats, clover, turnips, and so on. A principal part of the land is employed in tillage. The face of the country is rich, beautiful and picturesque; and it abounds with wood. It produces excellent cider; and the pastures are full of sheep, whose wool is of very fine quality. The principal rivers are the Wye, Munnow, Lug and Frome, all of which are well stocked with fish and salmon in particular. With a population of 113,878, it sends seven members to Parliament.

HEREFORD

The city of Hereford is pleasantly and commodiously situated among delightful meadows and rich corn-fields. It is almost encompassed by the Wye and two other rivers, over which are two bridges. It is a large place, and had six parish churches, but two of them were demolished in the civil wars. It also had a castle, which has long been destroyed. Hereford is a bishop's see, and the cathedral is a handsome structure. The chief manufacture is gloves, many of which are sent to London. The streets are broad and paved. It is 136 miles from London. There are markets on Wednesdays, Fridays and Saturdays. The population numbers 10,921.

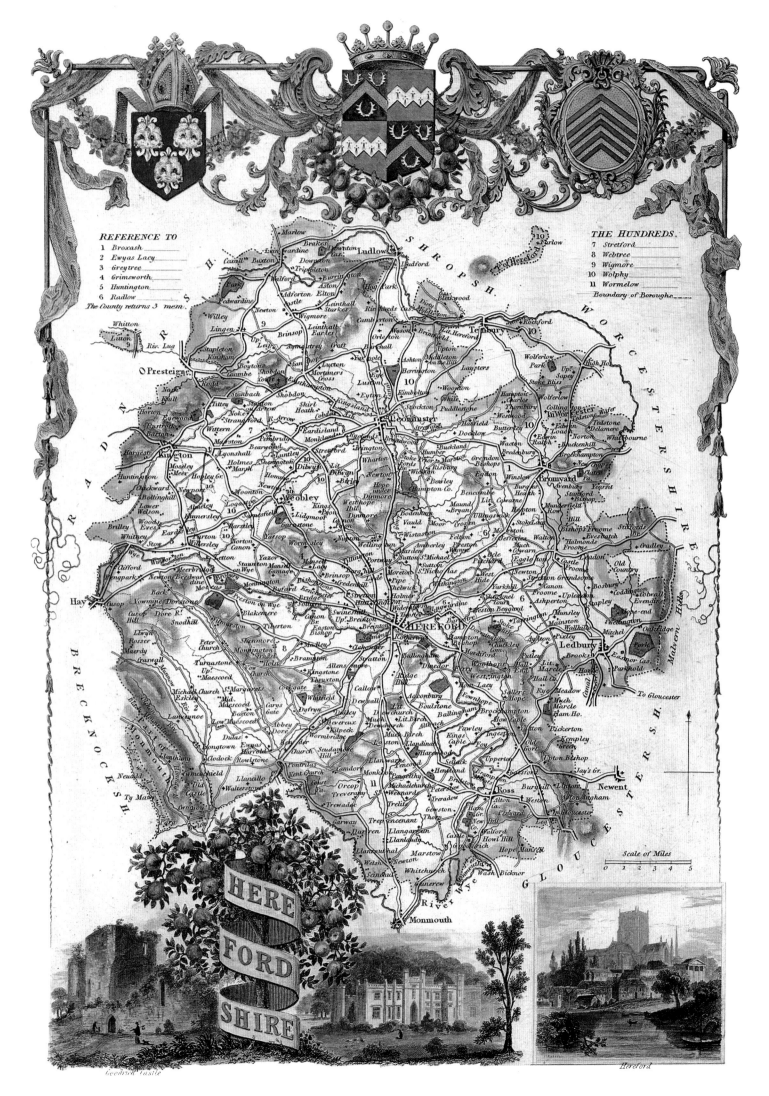

REFERENCE TO
1 Broxash
2 Ewyas Lacy
3 Greytree
4 Grimsworth
5 Huntington
6 Radlow
The County returns 3 mem.

THE HUNDREDS.
7 Stretford
8 Webtree
9 Wigmore
10 Wolphy
11 Wormelow
Boundary of Boroughs.

HEREFORD SHIRE

Goodrich Castle

Hereford

PLATE 4

WORCESTERSHIRE
Thomas Moule
The English Counties Delineated, 1837

Worcestershire is an English county, bounded by Warwickshire, Gloucestershire, Herefordshire, Staffordshire and Shropshire. It is about 35 miles in length and 30 in breadth; and contains 152 parishes and 12 market towns. Some parts are hilly, but it is generally level. The principal rivers are the Severn, the Avon, the Salwarp, the Teem and the Stour. The air is very healthy, and the soil in the vales and meadows very rich, producing corn and pastures; while several of the hills feed large flocks of sheep. The chief commodities of this county are corn, hops, wool, cloth, cheese, cider, perry and very fine salt. It has factories for pottery, iron, glass and so on and enjoys a good trade by canals. The population is 233,336, and it sends 12 members to Parliament.

WORCESTER

The city of Worcester is seated on the river Severn, over which is a beautiful stone bridge. The principal manufactured goods are horse-hair cloth, broad cloth, gloves and elegant china ware. There are nine parish churches, three grammar-schools, seven hospitals, an infirmary, a water-house and a well-contrived quay. The city is 111 miles from London. Markets are held on Mondays, Wednesdays and Fridays; and there is a considerable hop market on Saturdays. Fairs take place on the eve of Palm Sunday, the Saturday after Easter, August 15 and September 19. The population is 26,306.

SEVERN

One of the largest rivers in England, the Severn springs from Plinlimmon in Montgomeryshire, and, after a course of about 200 miles through the counties of Montgomery, Salop, Worcester and Gloucester, falls into the Bristol Channel. The Avon and the Wye are its chief tributaries. At its junction with the narrow sea it is about two miles across. The river is a channel of considerable trade, which is much increased by the canals. It is subject to a remarkable tidal phenomenon called the Bore.

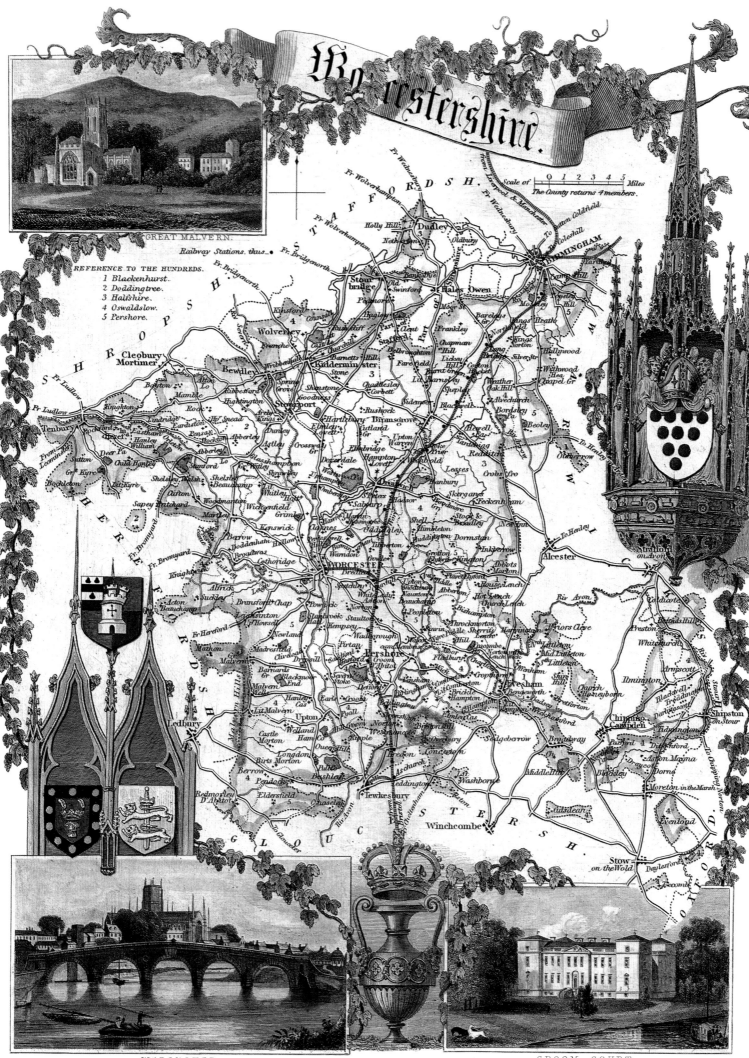

Worcestershire.

GREAT MALVERN.

Railway Stations, thus ▬

REFERENCE TO THE HUNDREDS.
1 Blackenhurst.
2 Doddingtree.
3 Halfshire.
4 Oswaldslow.
5 Pershore.

Scale of
0 1 2 3 4 5 Miles
The County returns 4 members.

WORCESTER.

CROOM COURT.

PLATE 5

WARWICKSHIRE

Thomas Moule
The English Counties Delineated, 1837

An English county, 50 miles in length and 35 in breadth, Warwickshire is bounded by Worcestershire, Oxfordshire, Gloucestershire, Northamptonshire, Leicestershire and Staffordshire. It contains 158 parishes and 17 market towns. The air is mild and healthful, and the soil fertile, producing corn and pastures, particularly in the southern part called the Vale of Red Horse. The county has few hills and is watered by the Avon, the Trent and their feeders. Coal, iron, lime and building-stone are abundant. It has some manufacturing industry and a good trade. The population numbers 401,715. It sends ten members to Parliament.

WARWICK

The chief town of the county, Warwick is seated on a rock near the River Avon. It was once fortified with a wall which is now in ruins, but it has still a strong and stately castle. It contains two parish churches, and in that of St. Mary's are several handsome tombs. The houses are well built, and the town principally consists of one regular built street, at each end of which is an ancient gate. It is adorned with a good free-school and a market-house. It enjoys a good trade, and is 91 miles from London. Markets are on Saturdays. The population numbers 9,775.

BIRMINGHAM

One of the largest of our manufacturing towns, Birmingham is finely and healthily situated on the slope of a hill, with a few small streams near it, which afterwards flow either to the North Sea, or by the Severn to the Atlantic. The coal and iron district terminates some miles from the town, and the strata in its vicinity are only sands, gravels and clays, whence the soil is very poor. The wealth of the town consists in its varied manufactured products, which include all kinds of steel and iron goods, from those made by the great rolling-mills to the most exquisitely finished ornaments, and steel pens, glass, silver goods and papier-mâché articles. There are several churches, built in a good style of architecture, and the newer parts of the town also are well built; the railway termini and some of the factories are also fine erections. King Edward's School has been rebuilt in a most elegant Gothic style, and the town-hall (which contains one of the noblest organs in Europe) is a grand building, constructed after the model of a Roman temple, and placed in a most commanding situation. A market is held on Thursdays. The population is 182,922.

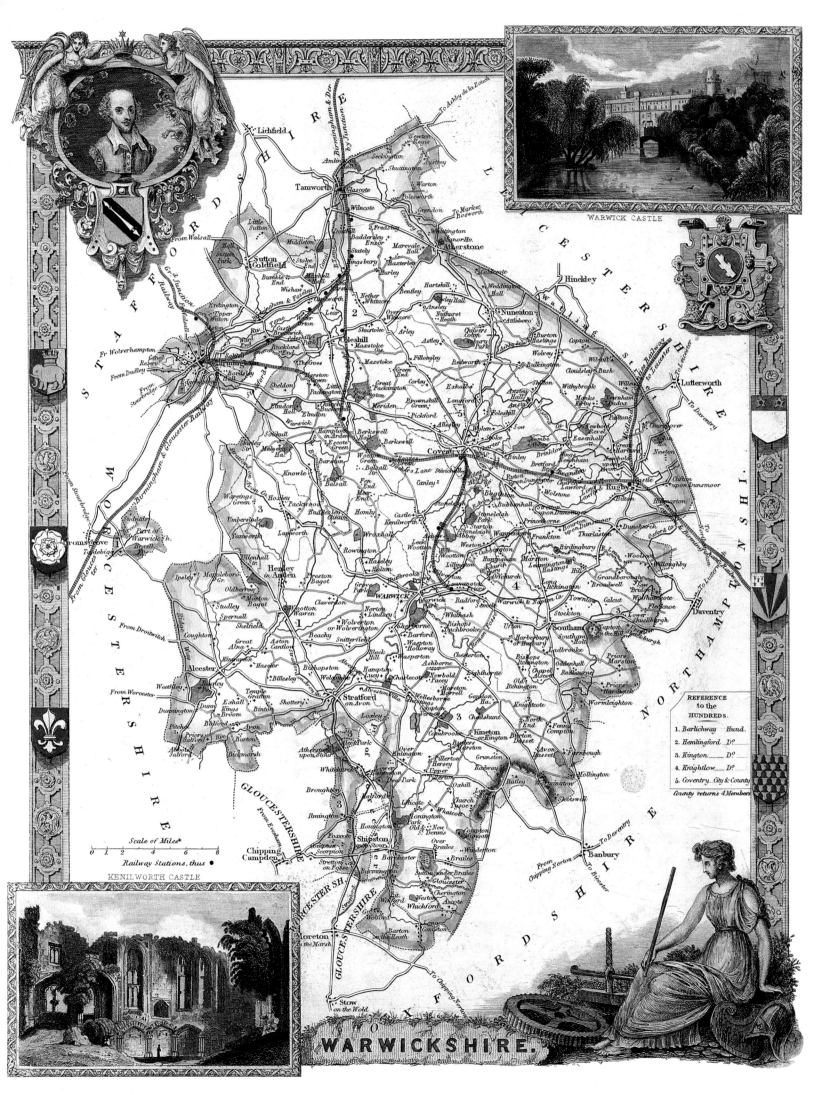

WARWICK CASTLE

KENILWORTH CASTLE

Scale of Miles
0 1 2 4 6 8
Railway Stations, thus ●

REFERENCE
to the
HUNDREDS.

1. Barlichway Hund.
2. Hemlingford D⁰
3. Kington D⁰
4. Knightlow D⁰
5. Coventry City & County

County returns 4 Members

WARWICKSHIRE.

STAFFORDSHIRE

LEICESTERSHIRE

WORCESTERSHIRE

NORTHAMPTONSHIRE

GLOUCESTERSHIRE

OXFORDSHIRE

WORCESTER SH.

Lichfield

Tamworth

Sutton Coldfield

Coleshill

Birmingham

Coventry

Nuneaton

Hinckley

Lutterworth

Daventry

Warwick

Henley in Arden

Alcester

Stratford on Avon

Southam

Banbury

Kineton or Kington

Shipston upon Stour

Chipping Campden

Moreton in the Marsh

Stow on the Wold

PLATE 6

MONMOUTHSHIRE

Thomas Moule

The English Counties Delineated, 1837

Monmouthshire is a county of England, lying on the Bristol Channel and bounded by Herefordshire, Brecknockshire, Gloucestershire and Glamorganshire. Its length is about 24 miles and its breadth 21. It contains seven market towns and 127 parishes. The air is temperate and healthy, and the soil fruitful, though mountainous and woody. The hills feed sheep, goats and horned cattle, and the valleys produce plenty of grass and corn. Beside the Wye, the Munnow and the Rhyney, or Rumney, this county contains almost the whole extent of the River Usk, which divides it into two unequal portions. The eastern and largest part is a tract fertile, on the whole, in corn and pastures and well wooded. It abounds with limestone, which is burnt on the spot for the general manure of the country. The smaller western portion is mountainous, and in great part unfavourable for cultivation; whence it is devoted to the feeding of sheep. It has several long narrow valleys, watered by streams that fall into the Bristol Channel. All the rivers above-mentioned, particularly the Wye and Usk, abound with fish, especially salmon and trout. Monmouthshire was formerly reckoned one of the counties of Wales, but since the reign of Charles II, it has been considered as an English county. The people use the Welsh language, but the English tongue is coming into use. The manufacture of this county is flannels. The population is 134,355. It sends four members to Parliament.

MONMOUTH

Pleasantly seated at the confluence of the rivers Wye, Munnow and Trothy, which almost surround it, Monmouth is a large handsome town and carries on a considerable trade with Bristol by the Wye. It is the county town and once had a stately castle, the remains of which show it to have been very strong. It is 128 miles from London. A market for corn and provisions is held on Saturdays. Fairs take place on Whitsun-Tuesday, September 4 and November 22. The population is 5,446.

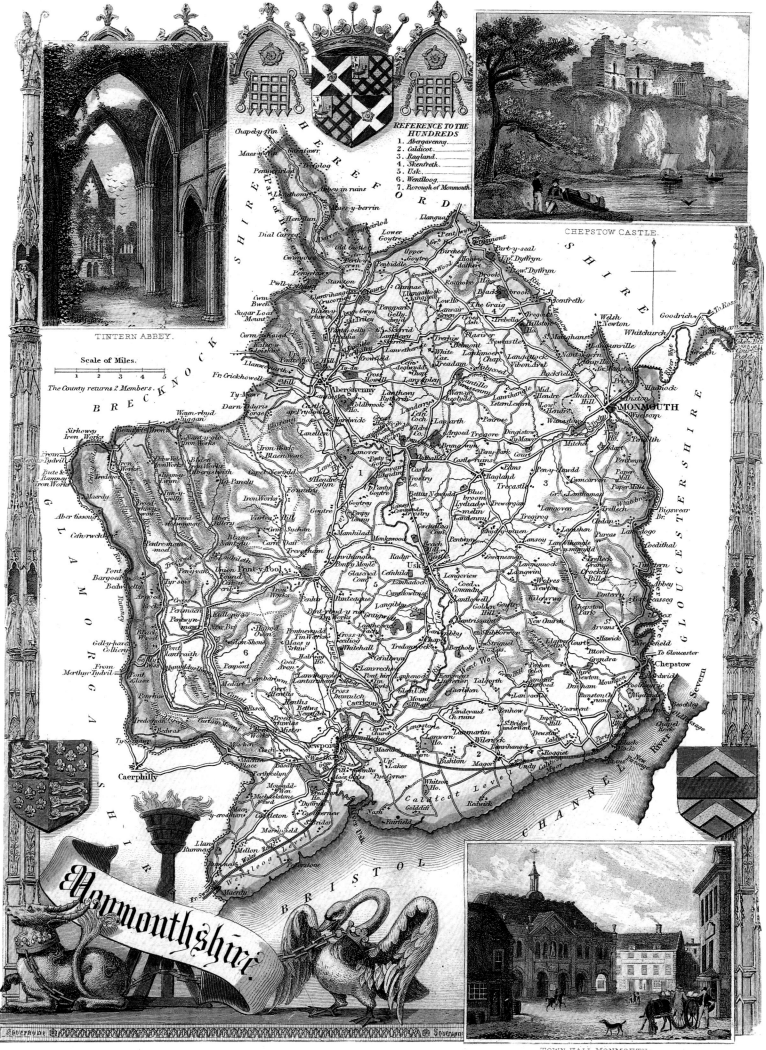

TINTERN ABBEY.

CHEPSTOW CASTLE.

REFERENCE TO THE
HUNDREDS
1. Abergavenny.
2. Caldicot.
3. Ragland.
4. Skenfreth.
5. Usk.
6. Wentlloog.
7. Borough of Monmouth

Scale of Miles.

The County returns 2 Members.

Monmouthshire

TOWN HALL MONMOUTH.

PLATE 7

GLOUCESTERSHIRE

Thomas Moule

The English Counties Delineated, 1837

Gloucestershire is a county of England, bounded by Monmouthshire, Herefordshire, Worcestershire, Warwickshire, Oxfordshire, Wiltshire and Somersetshire. It extends in length more than 60 miles, but is not more than 26 in breadth. It contains one city, 27 market towns, 280 parishes and 1,229 villages. The soil and appearance of this county vary in different parts, but the air is healthy throughout; sharp on the east or hilly part, which contains the Cotswold Hills, but mild in the rich vale of Severn, which occupies the centre. The west part, which is the smallest district, is varied by hill and dale, and chiefly occupied by the Forest of Dean, which was once full of oak trees, but now contains coal-mines and iron-works. The staple commodities are cheese, cider, perry, bacon, grain and fish, besides its factories of woollen cloths, hats, leather, paper, bar-iron, edge tools, nails, brass and so on. Its rivers are the Severn, the Warwickshire Avon, the Lower Avon, the Wye, Thames, Coln, Lech, Windrush, Evenlode, Churn, Leden, Swiliate, Caron and Stour. With a population of 431,383, it sends 15 members to Parliament.

GLOUCESTER

The chief city of the county, Gloucester contains five parish churches, besides its ancient and magnificent cathedral. The town is well built, and its four principal streets are greatly admired for the regularity of their junction in the centre of the town; besides which there are several smaller ones, all well paved. Here is a good stone bridge over the Severn, the lowest down that river, with a quay, wharf and custom-house. Gloucester is seated on the east side of the Severn, where, by its two streams, it forms the Isle of Alney. It is 106 miles from London. Markets are held on Wednesdays, fairs on April 5, July 5, September 28 and November 28, the latter chiefly for fat hogs. The population is 14,152.

CHELTENHAM

The town is noted for its mineral waters and for the extensive prospects from its adjoining hills. It is much improved of late years, with a new market-house and many handsome public buildings. It used to have a little trade from the neighbouring manufacturing towns, but now derives all its subsistence from its spa. It is 95 miles from London. Markets are on Thursdays. The population is 31,411.

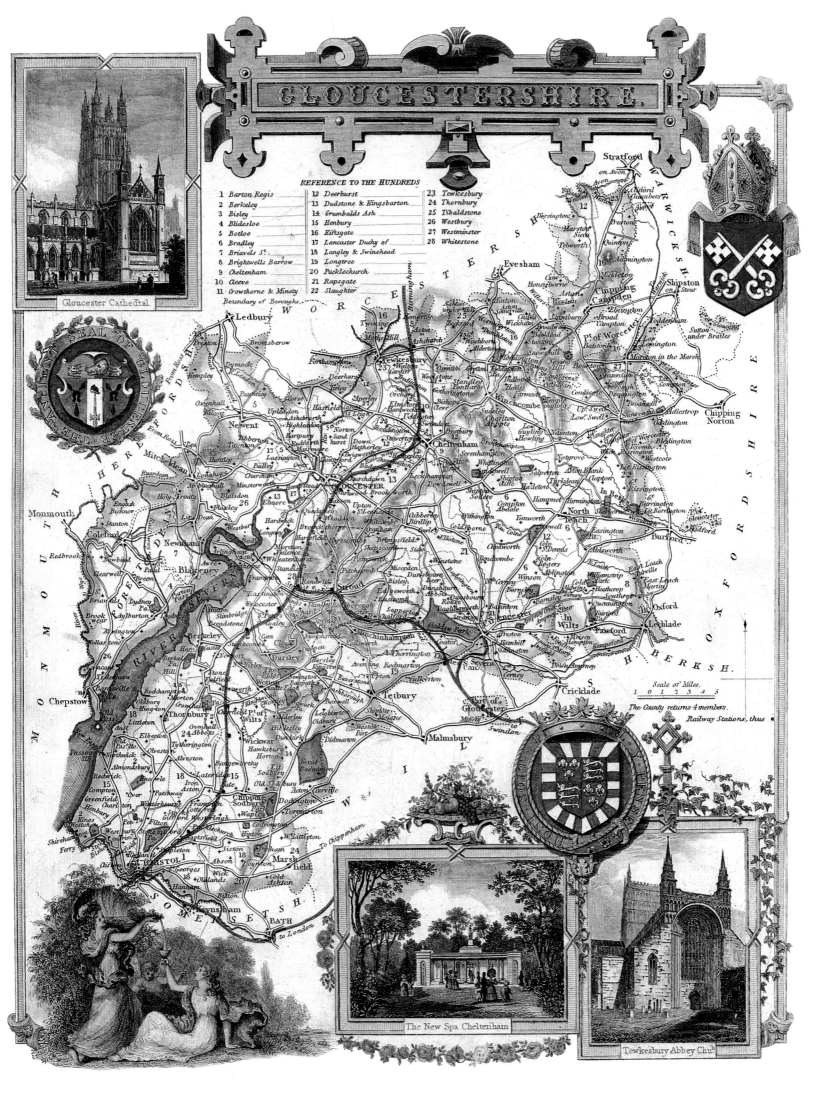

GLOUCESTERSHIRE.

REFERENCE TO THE HUNDREDS

1	Barton Regis	12	Deerhurst	23	Tewkesbury
2	Berkeley	13	Dudstone & Kingsbarton	24	Thornbury
3	Bisley	14	Grumbalds Ash	25	Tibaldstone
4	Blidesloe	15	Henbury	26	Westbury
5	Botloe	16	Kiftsgate	27	Westminster
6	Bradley	17	Lancaster Duchy of	28	Whitestone
7	Briavels St.	18	Langley & Swinehead		
8	Brightwells Barrow	19	Longtree		
9	Cheltenham	20	Pucklechurch		
10	Cleeve	21	Rapsgate		
11	Crowthorne & Minety	22	Slaughter		

Boundary of Boroughs

Scale of Miles.
1 0 1 2 3 4 5

The County returns 4 members.

Railway Stations, thus

Gloucester Cathedral.

The New Spa Cheltenham

Tewkesbury Abbey Chu:

PLATE 8

OXFORDSHIRE

Thomas Moule

The English Counties Delineated, 1837

A county of England, Oxfordshire is 47 miles in length and 29 in breadth. It is bounded by Buckinghamshire, Gloucestershire, Berkshire, Warwickshire and Northamptonshire, and has one city, 12 market towns, 280 parishes and 51 villages. The air is sweet, mild, pleasant and healthy, for which reason it contains several gentlemen's seats. The soil, though various, is fertile in corn and grass, and the hills are shaded with woods. It is also a great sporting country, there being an abundance of game preserved here. It has no manufacturing industry of any account, being chiefly agricultural. Its chief city is Oxford. The population is 161,643, and the county sends nine members to Parliament.

BANBURY

Banbury is a large, well-built town, and its markets are well served with provisions. It is the second town for beauty in the county, and seated on the river Charwell. The houses are generally built with stone, and the church is a large, handsome structure. Banbury has been long noted for its cakes and cheese, and is 78 miles from London. A market is held on Thursdays, and the population is 7,366.

BLENHEIM HOUSE AND PARK

The demesne and mansion in the neighbourhood of Oxford and Woodstock were given to the Duke of Marlborough for his brilliant successes in the war against the French. Blenheim House is named after a village lying on the Danube, near which the Duke and Prince Eugene, with the allied army, defeated the French and Bavarians, in August 1704.

OXFORD

For a description and town

plan of the city, see Plate 9, pages 26-27.

OXFORDSHIRE

BLENHEIM HOUSE.

RADCLIFFE LIBRARY.

Scale of Miles

Boundary of Boroughs
County returns 3 members.
Railway Stations thus ●

See Oxford lifts her Head sublime,
Majestic in the Moss of Time.
Nor wants there Graecia's better Part,
Mid the proud Isles of ancient Art.
Nor decent Doric to dispense
New Charms 'mid old Magnificence
And here and there soft Corinth weaves
Her dædal Coronet of Leaves;

WARTON's Ode

PLATE 9

OXFORD

Thomas Moule

The English Counties Delineated, 1837

Oxford is seated at the confluence of the Thames and Cherwell, on an eminence almost surrounded by meadows except on the eastern side. The whole town, with the suburbs, is of a circular form, three miles in circumference. It consists chiefly of two spacious streets, which cross each other in the middle of the town. It is chiefly celebrated for its university, which is said to have been founded by Alfred, but is generally supposed to have been of even earlier origin. Here are 20 colleges and five halls, several of which stand in the streets, and give the city an air of magnificence which has obtained for it the name of the City of Cathedrals. The colleges are very wealthy, but are retained exclusively by the Established Church. The number of students is usually about 2,000. Among the libraries in the university, the most distinguished is the Bodleian, founded by Thomas Bodley; also important are those of All Souls' College, Christ Church, Queen's, New College, St. John's, Exeter and Corpus Christi. Among other public buildings are the Theatre, the Ashmolean Museum, the Clarendon Printing-house, the Radcliffe Infirmary and a fine Observatory. Oxford is 58 miles from London. Markets are held on Wednesdays and Saturdays. The population is 23,834.

CHRIST CHURCH

One of the colleges of Oxford university, Christ Church was founded by Cardinal Wolsey in 1524, and remodelled by Henry VIII after the Cardinal's fall. It is a very noble institution and is immediately connected with the bishopric of Oxford, its chapel being the cathedral church, and the dean and chapter having the sole management of all its affairs. It has a good library. its buildings are on a very fine scale, and in the gate-way hangs the bell famed as Great Tom of Oxford.

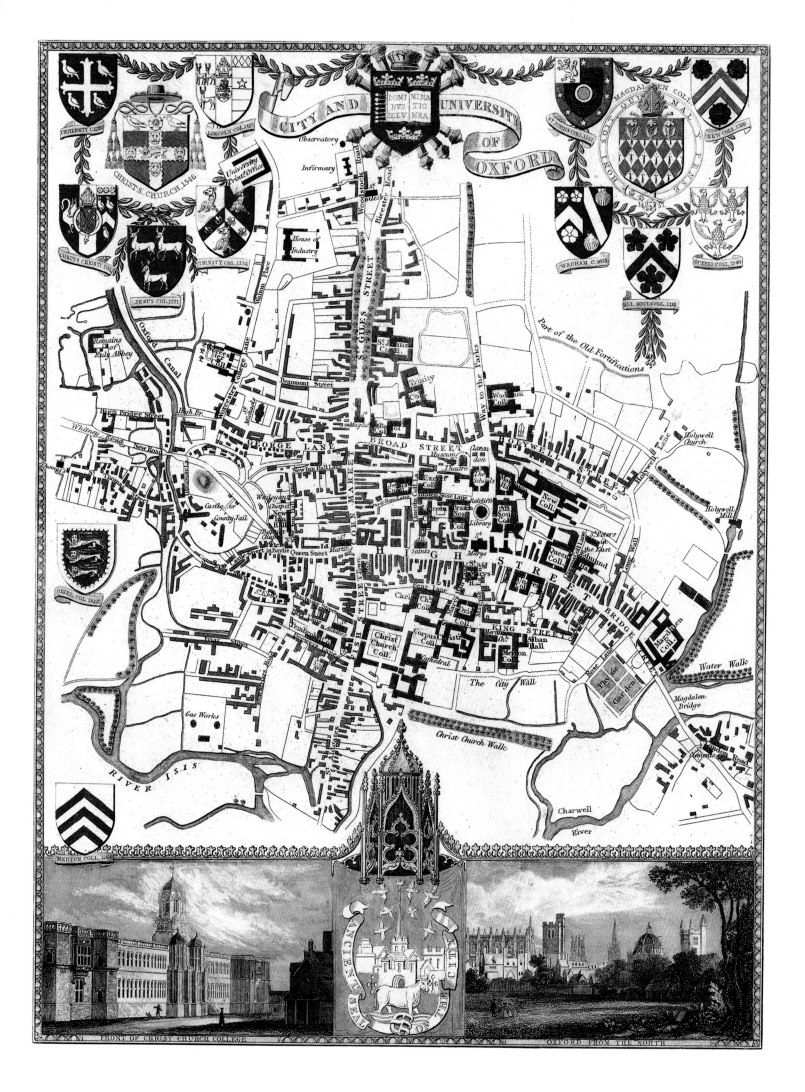

CITY AND UNIVERSITY OF OXFORD

DOMI NVS MINA
NVS TIO
ILLV MEA

UNIVERSITY C.1280
LINCOLN COL.1427
CHRIST'S CHURCH.1546
University Print. Office
CORPUS CHRISTI COLL.
TRINITY COL.1554
JESUS COL.1571

ST JOHN'S COLL.1557
MAGDALEN COLL
HONI SOIT QUI MAL Y PENSE
NEW COLL.1386
WADHAM C.1613
QUEEN'S COLL.1340
ALL SOULS COLL.1438

ORIEL COL.1325

MERTON COLL.1264

Observatory
Infirmary
House of Industry
Woodstock Road
Bicester Road
Remains of Rely Abbey
Oxford Canal
Worcester College Lane
Walton Place
Beaumont Street
High Bridge Street
High Br.
Whitney Road
New Road
St Michael
Magdalen Coll.
St Giles Street
St John's Coll.
Trinity Coll.
Way to the Parks
Wadham Coll.
Part of the Old Fortifications
Holywell Church
Holywell Street
Holywell Lane
George Lane
Broad Street
Museum
Theatre
Clarendon
New Inn Hall
Wesleyan Chapel
Castle or County Jail
Thomas's
Castle Street in Baylie
Queen Street
St Martins
St Mary's Hall
Jesus Coll.
Exeter Coll.
The Schools
Lincoln Coll.
Brazen Nose Coll.
Ratcliff Library
All Souls Coll.
High Street
Magdalen Hall
New Coll.
Holywell Mill
Long Wall
S.Peter's in the East
St Edmund
Queen's Coll.
Magdalen Bridge
Christ Ch. Coll.
Oriel Coll.
King Street
Corpus Christi Coll.
Alban Hall
Merton Coll.
The City Wall
Physic Garden
Water Walk
Magdalen Coll.
Christ Church Coll.
Cathedral
Christ Church Walk
Gas Works
London Road
Clements St.
RIVER ISIS
Charwell River

FRONT OF CHRIST CHURCH COLLEGE

ANCIENT SEAL OF THE CITY

OXFORD FROM THE NORTH

PLATE 10

SOMERSETSHIRE

Thomas Moule

The English Counties Delineated, 1837

Somersetshire is a county of England, lying on the Bristol Channel and bounded by Gloucestershire, Wiltshire, Dorsetshire and Devonshire. Its length is about 65 miles and its breadth between 30 and 40. It contains three cities, 33 market towns and 482 parishes. The air, in the lower grounds, is universally mild, and generally wholesome. The county is hilly, and the principal rivers are the Parret, Ivel, Chew, Axe, Thone, Brent, Exe, Frome and Avon. Coal and various metals, with good building and other kinds of stone, are found here. Corn and other crops are raised here; but cattle, sheep and cheese are more abundantly produced. Manufacture of several kinds of goods is carried on in its towns, and some places have a great trade. The population is 435,982. It sends 13 members to Parliament.

TAUNTON

The county town, Taunton, has long been the principal seat of the manufacture of coarse woollen goods, such as serges, corduroys, sagathies, druggets, shalloons and so on, though somewhat decayed of late years. It is seated on the River Thone, which is navigable hence to the Parret, and so to Bridgewater. The town is 144 miles from London and holds markets on Wednesdays and Saturdays. The population is 12,066.

GLASTONBURY

Glastonbury Abbey was formerly the most magnificent in the world, the domains and revenue of which were immense. It was anciently called the Isle of Avalon, into which no person, not even a bishop or prince, was allowed to enter without leave from the abbot, to whom this power was granted by Canute the Dane. Extensive ruins of this immense range of buildings are still remaining. The principal manufacture here is stockings. Nearly adjoining, on a high steep hill, is placed the tower of a church, called the Tor, which lifts its head into the clouds, and is an object of admiration to travellers and even serves as a landmark to seamen in the Bristol Channel. Glastonbury is situated in a low, marshy country, nearly encompassed with rivers, 129 miles from London. A market is held on Tuesdays, and the population numbers 3,314.

MENDIP HILLS

This range of hills in Somersetshire rises at its highest points to about 1,000 feet above the sea. They consist of mountain limestone and old red sandstone chiefly, and abound in combes, or narrow chasms, and caverns, in which many singular fossils have been found. Coal, copper, lead, galena and zinc are found in abundance. There is good pasturage for sheep and cattle on the sides of these hills.

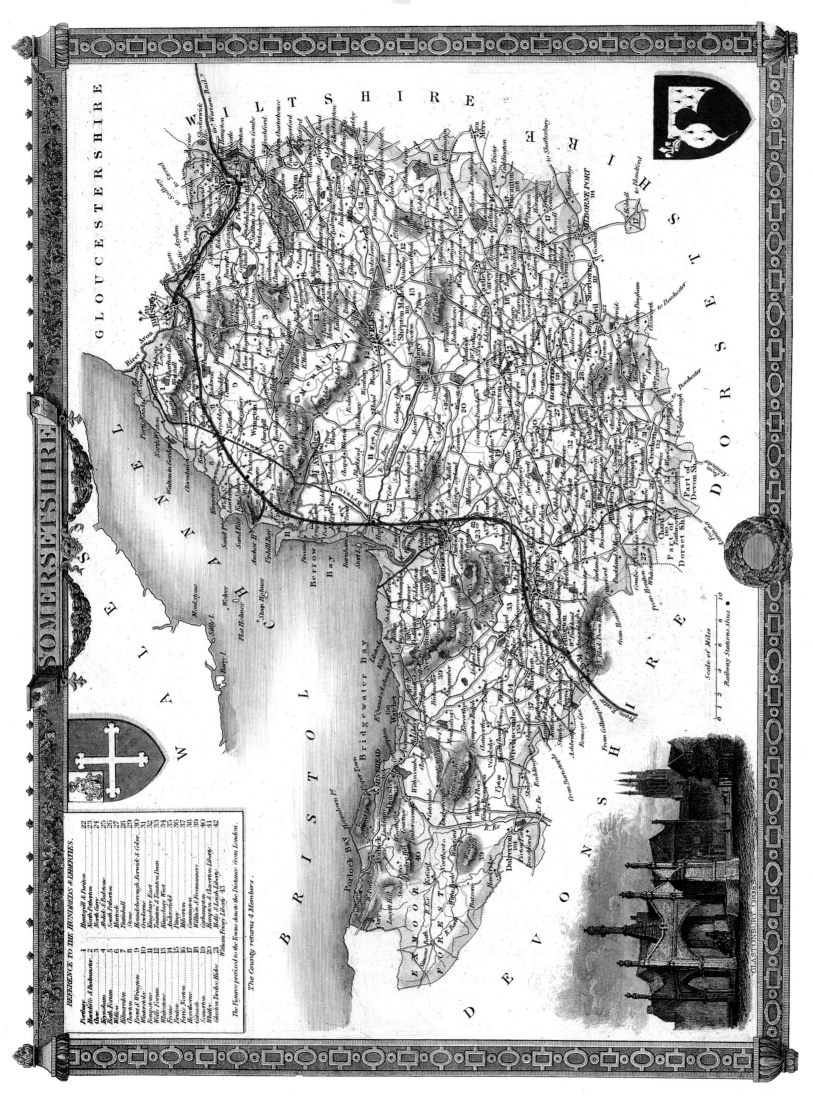

SOMERSETSHIRE

GLOUCESTERSHIRE

WILTSHIRE

DORSET

DEVONSHIRE

BRISTOL CHANNEL

Scale of Miles

Railway Stations, thus •

GLASTONBURY CROSS

PLATE 11

WILTSHIRE

Thomas Moule

The English Counties Delineated, 1837

An English county, bounded by Somersetshire, Gloucestershire, Berkshire, Hampshire and Dorsetshire, Wiltshire is 54 miles in length and 33 in breadth. It contains 304 parishes and 21 market towns. The principal rivers are the Willey, the Adder, the two Avons, the Thames and the Kennet. The air is generally good, though sharp upon the hills and downs in winter, but milder in the vales. The northern part is hilly, and the south level, and the middle full of downs, intermixed with valleys, wherein are rich meadows and corn-fields. There are several towns noted for woollen manufacture. Wiltshire abounds with relics of antiquity, the most interesting being ancient British earth-works, temples and tombs. The county has a population of 258,733 and sends 18 members to Parliament.

SALISBURY

Salisbury or New Sarum is pleasantly situated on the river Avon, that waters most of the principal streets, which are large and spacious. It has several handsome buildings, particularly the cathedral, which is a stately, handsome building, with a lofty spire. Its chief trade arises from silk manufacture. It is 80 miles from London. Markets are held on Tuesdays and Saturdays. The population is 10,086.

STONEHENGE

Stonehenge is the most remarkable Druidical ruin of Great Britain. It is situated on Salisbury Plain, about six miles from Salisbury, on the summit of a gently rising hill. The monument consists of a vast circular entrenchment, over 100 yards in diameter, in the centre of which is a great accumulation of huge masses of rock, some standing upright and having other pieces laid transversely across them, but mostly prostrate. In spite of this disorder, it is clear that the rocks are the relics of a temple, which consisted of a double circle of upright stones, the outermost being by far the largest and connected by the transverse pieces into one continuous circular enclosure. Within the smaller circle were five pairs of upright stones, with the transverse pieces connecting them in pairs, about 20 feet in height. Before the centre one was a flat stone which seems to have been the altar. Beside these, there are several others within the circles, or between them and the embankment, and the whole number of them is 97. Most of them are of the kind of stone called gray-weathers and were evidently quarried in the neighbourhood. Legends in abundance remain respecting the use and the erection of these stones, and one is embodied in the common name it bears among the Welsh, the dance of the Giants. Antiquaries and mechanicians have vainly endeavoured to show how, with the rude engines of the ancient Britons, such enormous masses could be quarried, transported and erected here.

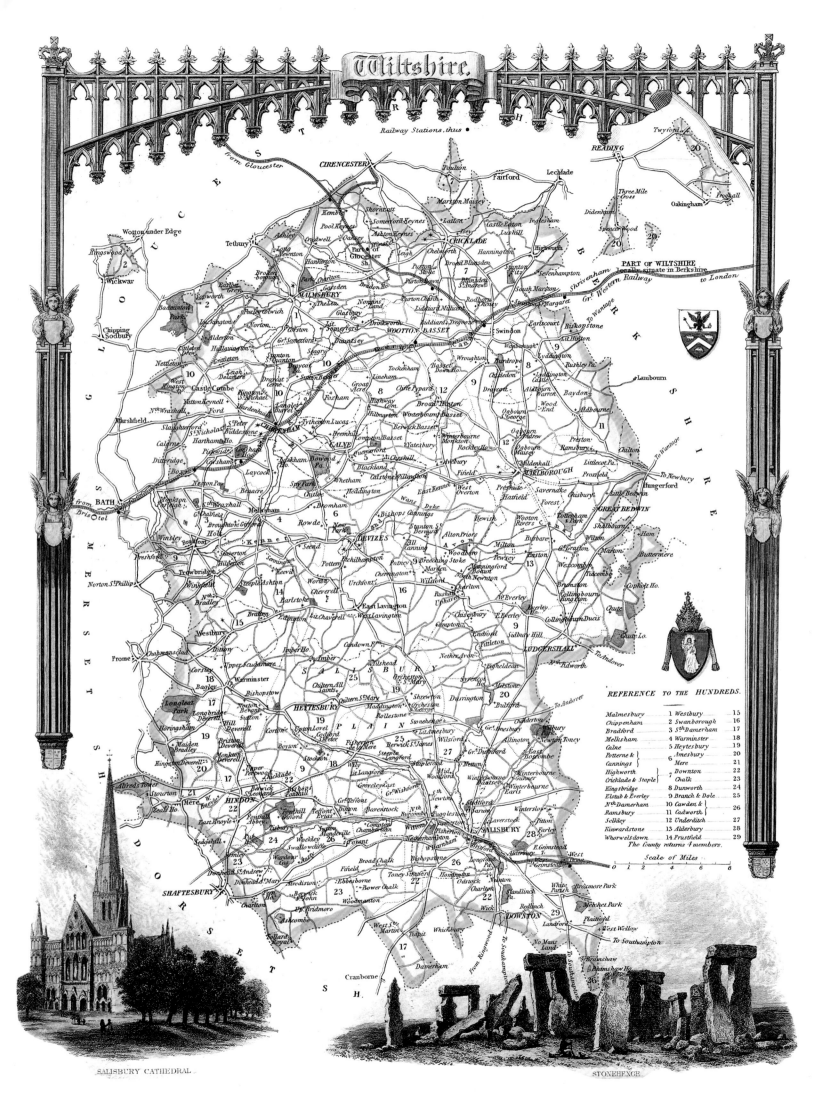

Wiltshire.

Railway Stations, thus •

Scale of Miles
0 1 2 4 6 8

SALISBURY CATHEDRAL.

STONEHENGE.

PLATE 12

BERKSHIRE

Thomas Moule

The English Counties Delineated, 1837

The English county of Berkshire is bounded on the north by Oxfordshire and Buckinghamshire, on the west by Wiltshire, on the south by Hampshire and Surrey and on the east by Middlesex and Buckinghamshire. It is about 40 miles long and 25 broad. A great chalk range, which rises to almost 900 feet in height at White Horse Hill, runs nearly due west through it. The county has good pastures on these hills, and the lower land is fertile and woody. The Thames is its chief river; others include the Kennet, the Loddon and the Auburn. It is mainly an agricultural county; but some woollen cloth is manufactured. The White Horse Hill and Vale are so named from the figure of a horse rudely made on the side of the chalk hill by cutting away the turf from the chalk below. The horse is nearly 400 feet long, and may be seen for many miles; it is believed to be of great antiquity. Reading, Abingdon, Windsor and Wallingford are the chief towns in Berkshire. It returns nine members to Parliament and has a population of 161,147.

READING

Pleasantly set on the river Kennet, near its confluence with the Thames, Reading has several bridges. The newer parts of the town are tolerably well built, and there are several public edifices, which greatly ornament it. It also has some interesting ruins. It has a good trade. The town has several valuable manufactures, beside being an emporium for corn, malt and so on. Canal and railroad offer great facilities for the transport of its commodities. It is 39 miles from London. There are markets on Saturdays (for corn) and Mondays (for cattle), and fairs on February 2, May 1, July 25 and September 21. The population is 18,937.

WINDSOR

Windsor is pleasantly situated on the banks of the Thames, in a healthful air, and is a handsome, large and well-inhabited place; but chiefly famous for its magnificent castle, which is a royal palace. The castle is surrounded by a fine park, in which is the beautiful artificial lake, called Virginia Water. Windsor is 22 miles from London. A market is held on Saturdays. The population of the whole town numbers 7,528; of Old Windsor, 1,600.

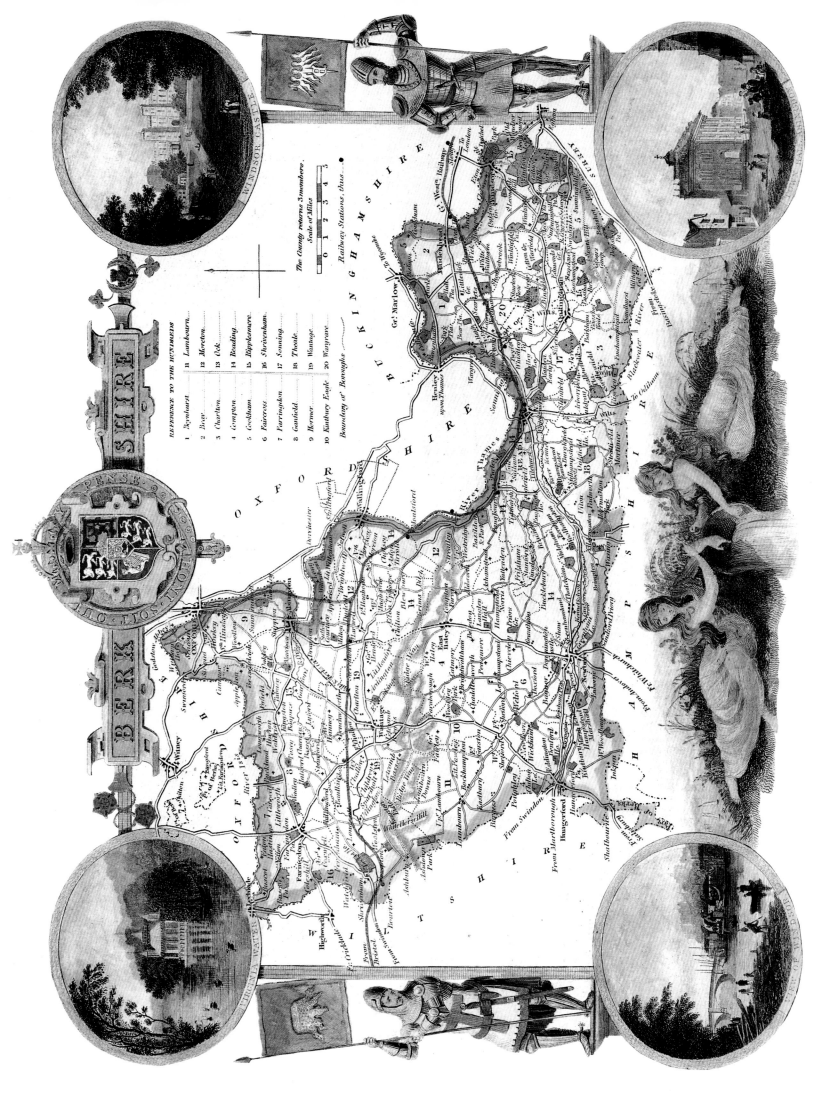

PLATE 13

CORNWALL

Thomas Moule

The English Counties Delineated, 1837

The English county of Cornwall forms the south-west extremity of Great Britain. It is bounded on the east by Devonshire; its other parts are washed by the sea. Its length from east to west is 74 miles and its greatest breadth is about 43. On the south-west it terminates in two promontories, the Lizard Point and the Land's End. It contains 206 parishes. The central part, which is the highest, is mostly covered with barren moors, but there are fertile tracts beside the rivers which flow to the north and south of it. The Tamar, the Camel, the Fowey and the Fal are its chief streams. Being surrounded on three sides by the sea, the county keeps its temperature very even, there being seldom any severe frosts or great heats, and spring being earlier here than in the rest of England; but it is exposed to storms, and has an abundance of rainy and foggy weather. Its chief importance arises from its mineral riches. Cornwall has valuable copper mines, in which gold and silver are sometimes met with in small quantities. Its tin mines are most extensive, and have been celebrated since remotest antiquity. Lead, iron, zinc and arsenic also occur. There are very many kinds of rock quarried here, including granite and freestone for building, slates for roofing and grit for making mill-stones. A species of very clear crystal is common, which is known to jewellers as the Cornish diamond. The growth of corn is not considerable for its extent, nor the numbers of cattle. Cornwall was one of the retreats of the ancient Britons when the Saxons seized the east parts of the island, and it is but lately that the last remnant of the old Celtic dialect of this island has become extinct. The county gives a ducal title to the eldest son of the sovereign; and as revenue, he has the proceeds of a duty charged on all the tin raised. With a population of 341,279, it returns 14 members to Parliament.

BODMIN

Bodmin is seated in a dip between two high hills, which renders the air very unwholesome. It consists chiefly of one street, and the many decayed houses show it was once a place of greater note; it formerly had the privilege of the coinage of tin. It is 334 miles from London. Markets are held on Saturdays. The population is 4,643.

LAUNCESTON

Launceston formerly had a monastery and a noble castle, because of its strength called Castle Terrible, the lower part of which is now made use of for the gaol. The town is seated on the River Tamar. It is 214 miles from London. Markets are held on Thursdays and Saturdays. The population is 2,460.

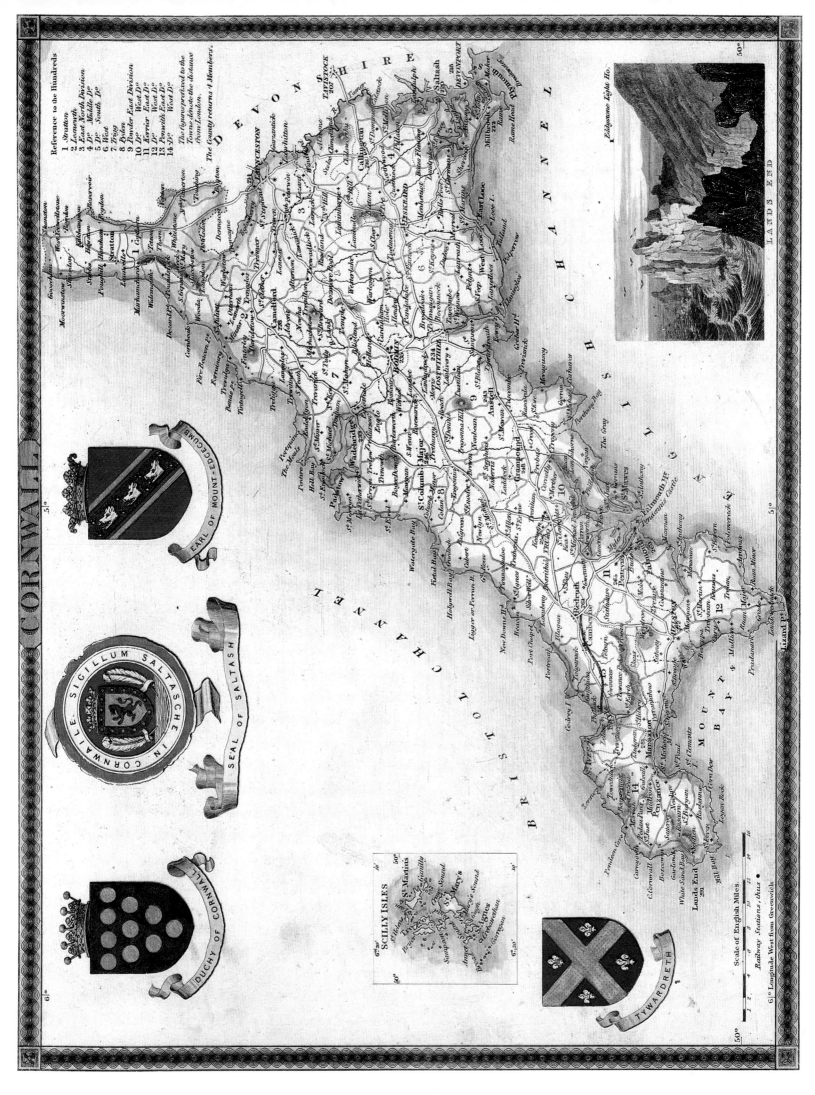

CORNWALL

Reference to the Hundreds

1 Stratton
2 Lesnewth
3 East North Division
4 D°. Middle D°.
5 D°. South D°.
6 West
7 Trigg
8 Pyder
9 Powder East Division
10 D°. West D°.
11 Kerrier East D°.
12 D°. West D°.
13 Penwith East D°.
14 D°. West D°.

The figures prefixed to the Towns denote the distance from London.

The County returns 4 Members.

EARL OF MOUNT-EDGCUMB

SIGILLUM SALTASCHE IN CORNWALE

SEAL OF SALTASH

DUCHY OF CORNWALL

TYWARDRETH

SCILLY ISLES

Scale of English Miles.

Railway Stations, thus

6½° Longitude West from Greenwich

LANDS END

Eddystone Light Ho.

DEVONSHIRE

BRISTOL CHANNEL

ENGLISH CHANNEL

MOUNT'S BAY

PLATE 14

DEVONSHIRE

Thomas Moule

The English Counties Delineated, 1837

Devonshire is a county of England, reaching from the Bristol to the English Channel, and bounded by Cornwall, Somersetshire and Dorsetshire. It is 69 miles in length, and 60 in breadth. The country is very hilly and abounds in huge granite rocks, some of whose peaks are above 1,500 feet in height. The highland is covered with wide moors, of which Dartmoor is the most extensive. But in the valleys and lower ground the soil is fertile. Its principal rivers are the Exe, the Culm, the Dart, the Tamar and the Otter. Some parts of its coasts are composed of lofty cliffs, but at others there is a beautiful sandy shore. The air and climate are so mild and salubrious that invalids often retire to its sea-ports for the winter. Limestone, granite, some building-stone and a species of wood-coal are found here, as well as some kinds of variegated marble. It produces corn and other crops, and fruit trees, especially apples, whence much cider is made. Its fisheries also are of value. It has a population of 533,460 and sends 22 members to Parliament.

PLYMOUTH AND DEVONPORT

Plymouth is a large sea-port, seated between the mouths of the rivers Plym and Tamar, and one of the chief naval magazines in the kingdom, owing to its excellent port or harbour, which is capable of safely containing 1,000 sail. There are, properly speaking, however, three harbours, Catwater, Sutton Pool and Hamoaze. The first is the mouth of the Plym, and affords a safe and commodious harbour for merchant ships, but is seldom entered by ships of war. The second is frequented by merchant ships only and is almost surrounded by the houses of the town. The third inlet, which is the mouth of the Tamar, is the harbour for the reception of the British navy. The town has a good herring fishery, and a considerable trade beside its manufactures, which are of all kinds of goods required in shipping; and the great business arising from the dockyard. It is 210 miles from London. Markets are on Mondays, Tuesdays and Saturdays. The population is 37,058. Devonport stands at the mouth of the Tamar, and is well fortified, with a noble dockyard and arsenal for the navy. Its old name was Plymouth Dock. It is 210 miles from London and has a population of 33,820.

EXETER

For a description and town

plan of the city, see Plate 15, pages 38-39.

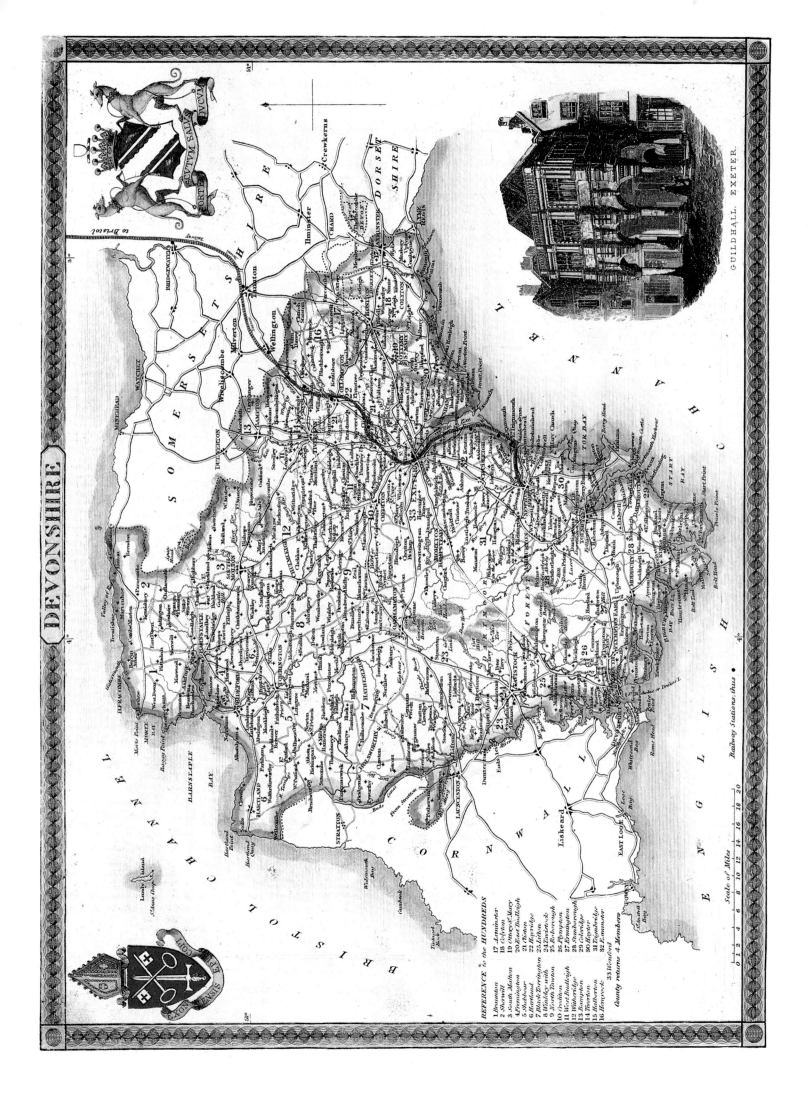

DEVONSHIRE

GUILDHALL, EXETER.

Scale of Miles

Railway Stations, thus •

PLATE 15

EXETER

G. Cole and J. Roper

*The British Atlas: Comprising a Complete Set of
County Maps of England and Wales; with a General Map of
Navigable Rivers and Canals; and Plans of Cities
and Principal Towns,* 1801 and later.

The county town of Devon, Exeter is an ancient city. It is situated on the eastern bank of the River Exe, about nine miles north of the English Channel. This place was called by the Saxons 'Monkton' from the number of religious establishments it contained. The ancient walls of the city included a space of ground four furlongs in length and three in breadth, and the area is intercepted by four principal streets, which meet near the centre and diverge at right angles to connect the city with the suburbs. In 1769, the walls were standing, but many parts of them have since been taken down. The principal street, called High Street, has the appearance of antiquity, as have many of the buildings in different parts of the city; but within the last half century handsome edifices and new streets have been erected, some of which would not suffer from comparison with those in most other parts of the kingdom.

There is a handsome stone bridge over the Exe, erected some fifteen years since, at the expense of nearly £20,000. In 1675, a canal was cut from Topsham to Exeter: the first canal carried out in the United Kingdom for the purpose of enabling sea-going vessels to pass to an inland port. By means of sluices and floodgates vessels of 150 tons burden are admitted to a good quay near the city walls.

The manufacture of coarse woollen goods has been carried on here very extensively, but it has much decayed of late years. Vast quantities of duroys and serges used to be exported to Spain, Portugal and the Mediterranean, to the estimated amount of £600,000 annually, but though these and other markets have failed, the demand for these articles is still considerable. Exeter is 171 miles from London and has a population of 17,388.

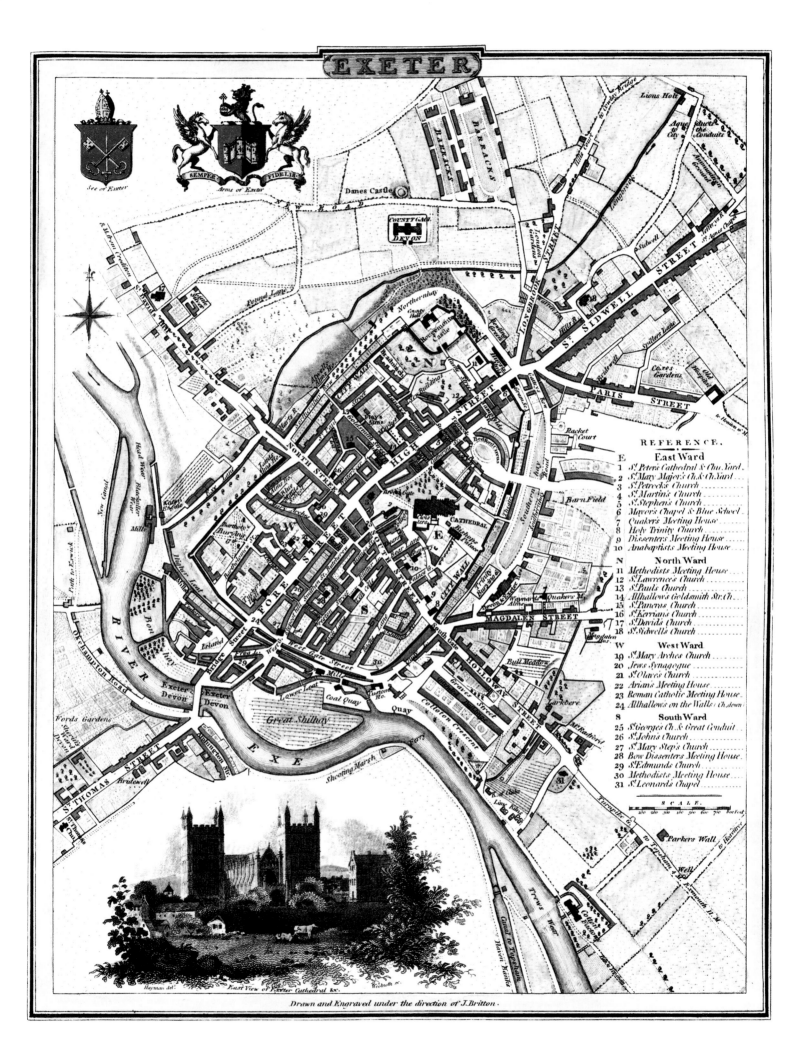

EXETER

See of Exeter

SEMPER FIDELIS
Arms of Exeter

REFERENCE.

E   **East Ward**
1   St Peter's Cathedral & Chu. Yard
2   St Mary Major's Ch. & Ch. Yard
3   St Petrock's Church
4   St Martin's Church
5   St Stephen's Church
6   Mayer's Chapel & Blue School
7   Quaker's Meeting House
8   Holy Trinity Church
9   Dissenters Meeting House
10   Anabaptists Meeting House

N   **North Ward**
11   Methodists Meeting House
12   St Lawrence's Church
13   St Pauls Church
14   Allhallow's Goldsmith Str. Ch.
15   St Pancras Church
16   St Kerrian's Church
17   St David's Church
18   St Sidwell's Church

W   **West Ward**
19   St Mary Arches Church
20   Jews Synagogue
21   St Olave's Church
22   Arian's Meeting House
23   Roman Catholic Meeting House
24   Allhallows on the Walls (Ch. down)

S   **South Ward**
25   St Georges Ch. & Great Conduit
26   St John's Church
27   St Mary Step's Church
28   Bow Dissenters Meeting House
29   St Edmunds Church
30   Methodists Meeting House
31   St Leonard's Chapel

SCALE.

Hayman del.   East View of Exeter Cathedral &c.   Woolnoth sc.

Drawn and Engraved under the direction of J. Britton.

PLATE 16

DORSETSHIRE

Thomas Moule
The English Counties Delineated, 1837

A county of England lying on the English Channel, Dorsetshire is bounded by Devonshire, Somersetshire, Wiltshire and Hampshire. It is about 52 miles in length and 36 in breadth, and contains 248 parishes. A range of hills belonging to the chalk formation crosses the county, some of which are above 500 feet in height. It is watered by the Stour, the Frome, the Ivel and various smaller rivers. Parts of the coast are precipitous, and there are some good harbours. Portland Point is at low water connected with the main-land by a long narrow spit of sand. Very good building-stone is obtained here. The greater part of the county is laid down in pasture, the chalk downs affording excellent sheep-walks. The fisheries are also valuable. Dorsetshire has both linen and woollen manufactures. The population is 175,043. It returns 14 members to Parliament.

DORCHESTER

The county town of Dorsetshire, Dorchester is a town of great antiquity, and stands by the river Frome. The houses are well built, and it has three handsome streets. It is a corporate and assize town. It has but little trade. It is 120 miles from London. Markets are held on Wednesdays and Saturdays. The population numbers 3,249.

PORTLAND

This peninsula near Weymouth is nearly seven miles round, and exceedingly strong both by nature and art. It is surrounded by inaccessible rocks, except at the landing-place, where there is a strong castle. The whole peninsula is one continuous mass of oolitic rock. The town is small. But the area includes several small hamlets. It is 132 miles from London. The population is 2,852.

DORSETSHIRE.

Scale of Miles

DORCHESTER

SEAL OF THE ABBEY

SEAL OF Sᵗ EDWARDS

ABBEY SHAFTESBURY.

SHAFTESBURY.

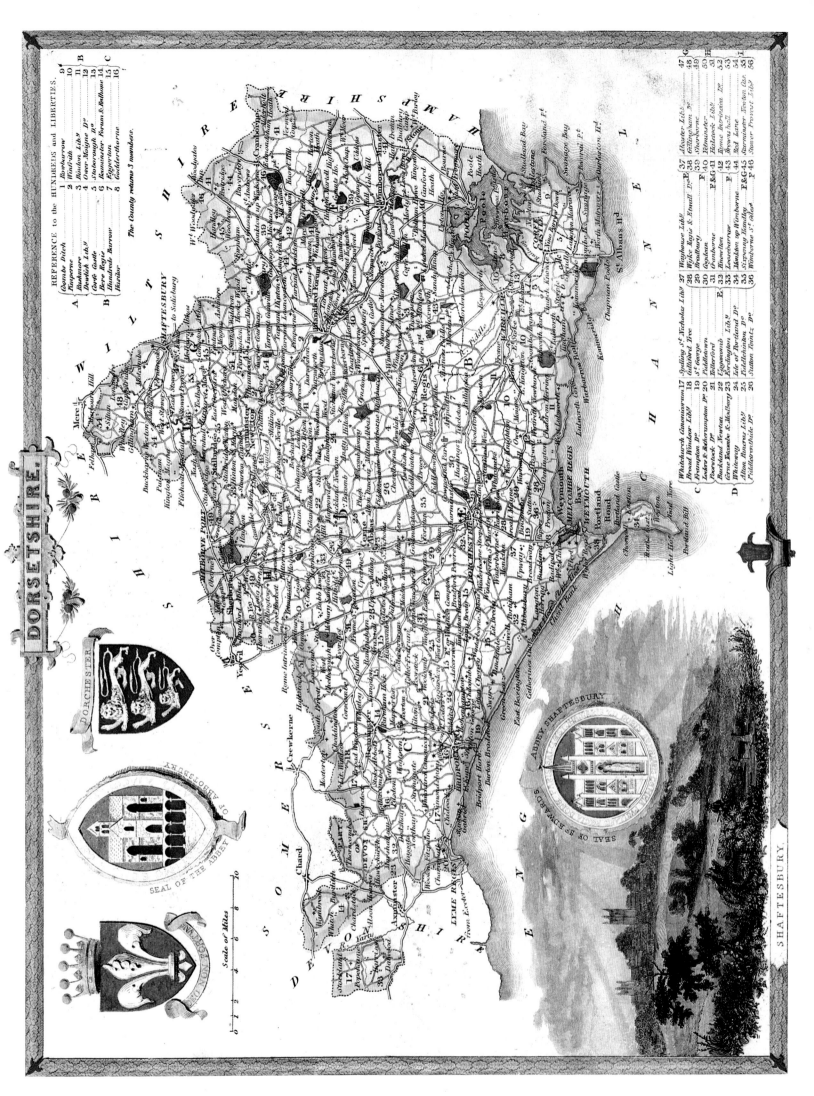

PLATE 17

HAMPSHIRE

Thomas Moule

The English Counties Delineated, 1837

Hampshire is a county of England, lying on the English Channel and bounded by Dorsetshire, Wiltshire, Berkshire, Surrey and Sussex. Excluding the Isle of Wight, it extends for 42 miles in length and 38 in breadth. It contains one city, 20 market towns, 253 parishes and 1,062 villages. Hampshire is one of the most fertile counties in England. A range of chalk downs runs through the north part of the county. The county's products are the finest corn and hops, very large flocks of cattle and sheep, with excellent wool, bacon, honey and timber. For the last it has been particularly famous on account of its great woods, of which the principal are the New Forest and the Forest of East Bere. The principal rivers are the Avon, the Test or Tese, the Itchen and the Stour. With a population of 355,004, Hampshire returns 19 members to Parliament.

WINCHESTER

Winchester, the county town, stands on the Itchin, and has six parish churches in addition to the cathedral, which is a large and beautiful structure, and in which are interred several Saxon kings and queens. The other remarkable buildings are the bishop's palace, the hall where the assizes are kept and the college or school, which last is without walls. The city is 62 miles from London. There are markets on Wednesdays and Saturdays. The population numbers 10,732.

PORTSMOUTH

Portsmouth is situated on the island of Portsea and is very strongly fortified. The royal docks and yards resemble distinct towns, under a government separate from the garrison. The harbour is one of the finest in the world, as there is water sufficient for the largest ships; and it is so very capacious that the whole English navy could ride here in safety. Across the harbour's mouth, a floating steam-bridge plies continually between this town and Gosport. The town is extensive, and has some fine streets and public walks. It is 72 miles from London. Markets are held on Tuesdays, Thursdays and Saturdays. The population of Portsmouth is 9,354, and of Portsea 43,678.

ISLE OF WIGHT

*For a description and map of
the island, see Plate 18, pages 44-45.*

SOUTHAMPTON

*For a description and town
plan of the city, see Plate 19, pages 46-47.*

HAMPSHIRE

REFERENCE
to the
HUNDREDS & LIBERITIES.

Northern Division   Southern Division.
1 Andover .... Hd   1 Bosmere .... Hd
2 Wherwell .... Do   2 East Meon .. Do
3 Thorngate .. Do   3 Finch. Dean. Do
4 Kings Sombourn Do   4 Hambledon Do
5 Barton Stacy .. Do   5 Meon Stoke Do
6 Buddly .... Do   6 Bp. Waltham. Do (part of)
7 Evingar .... Do   7 Havant Lib.
8 Kingsclere .. Do   8 Portsdown .. Hd
9 Overton .... Do   9 Fareham .. Do
10 Eastrow .... Do   10 Titchfield. .. Do
11 Basingstoke Do   11 Mansbridge. Do
12 Bermondspit Do   12 Bishleu. Lib.
13 Crondall .... Do   13 Bishops Sutton. Do
14 Holdshot .... Do   14 Bp. Waltham Hd (part of)
15 Odiham .... Do   15 New Forest. Hd
16 Micheldever. Do   16 Fordingbridge. Do
17 Alresford New Lib.   17 Breamore Lib.
18 Alton .... Do   18 Ringwood. .. Hd
19 Bishops Sutton. Do   19 Christchurch Do
20 Selborne .... Do   20 Beaulieu. Lib.
21 Bountisborough Do   21 Alverstoke & .. Lib.
22 Buddlesgate. Do   21 Gosport. Lib.
23 Fawley .... Do   22 W. Medina Do
24 Mansborough Do   23 E. Medina Do

This sign ✻ denotes that, that part of the
Hundred belongs to the Hundred having the
same sign and figure although in a different
Division.

The County returns 4 members.
Railway Stations thus ⏺

DUKE OF WELLINGTON

VIRTUTIS FORTUNA COMES

PETERSFIELD

PORTSMOUTH

SOUTHAMPTON

SOUTHWICK

WINCHESTER

SOUTHAMPTON

Scale of English Miles.

PLATE 18

ISLE OF WIGHT
Thomas Moule
The English Counties Delineated, 1837

An island belonging to Hampshire, and separated from it by a narrow channel called the Solent Sea, the Isle of Wight is about 20 miles long and 12 broad. It is crossed by a range of chalk hills, none exceeding 700 feet in height; and has a rather high level on the south side, one point being above 800 feet in elevation, but on the north side is lower and more level. It has some most romantic scenery amongst its hills. At the western extremity are those remarkable detached masses of chalk called the Needles. It has a rich soil, and produces corn, and other crops abundantly. The beauty of the scenery and its agreeable climate make it a favourite resort for invalids and pleasure-takers. To the geologist it offers some very remarkable studies. Cowes is its principal place of maritime trade, and Newport its chief town. The population is 42,550.

COWES

Cowes is a sea-port on the north coast of the Isle of Wight, divided by the river Meden, or Medina. It is a place of good trade, resorted to by merchant-ships waiting for convoy and passage-boats to and from Portsmouth and Southampton, and is the station of the packet carrying the mail from the island to London. Its population is 4,987.

NEWPORT

Newport is called in Latin, Medina, from whence the whole island, on the east and west sides of it, is called East and West Medina. It is situated almost in the centre of the island, on the river Cowes (which falls seven miles below it into the sea, and which is navigable up to the quay here for small vessels), 91 miles from London. The population numbers 3,858.

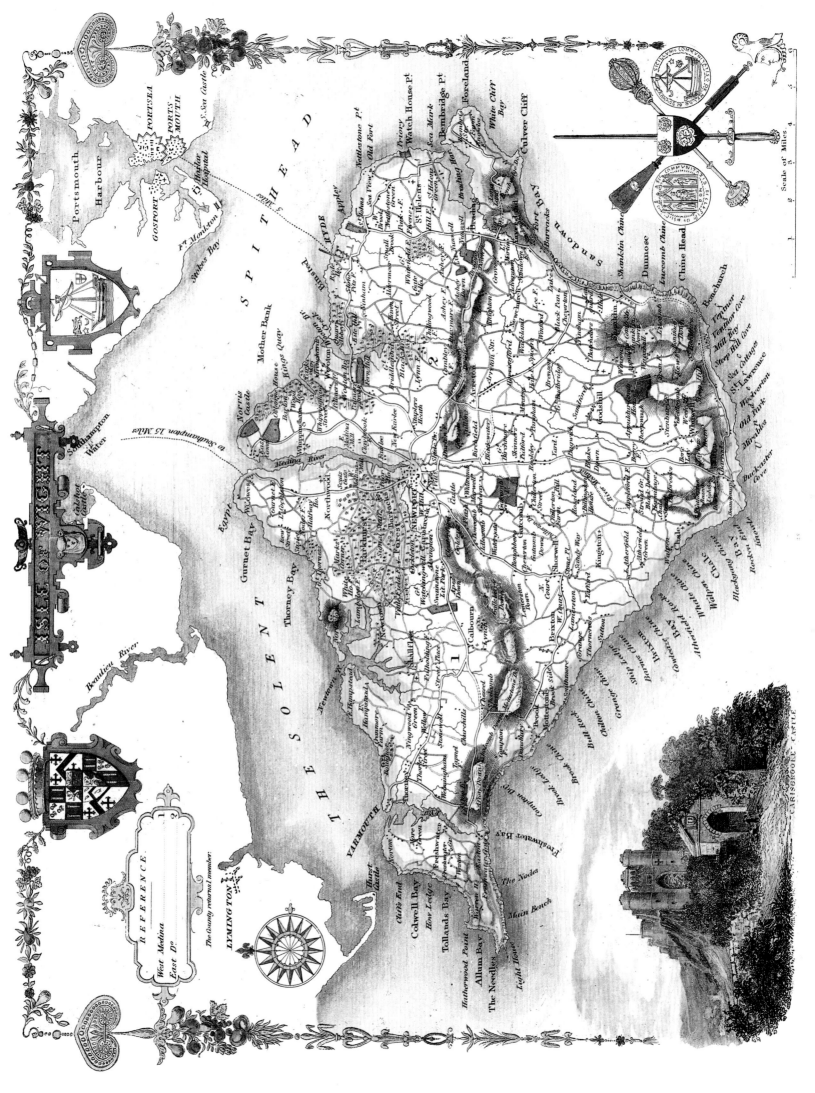

ISLE OF WIGHT

REFERENCE.
West Medina
East Do

The County returns 1 member.

Scale of Miles.

CARISBROOKE CASTLE.

THE SOLENT

SPITHEAD

Portsmouth Harbour

PORTSEA
PORTS-MOUTH
GOSPORT
St Sea Castle
Haslar Hospital
Ft Monkston

Stokes Bay

Mother Bank

Southampton Water
to Southampton 15 Miles
Beaulieu River

LYMINGTON

Hurst Castle
Cliff End
Colwell Bay
How Ledge
Tallands Bay
Hatherwood Point
Alum Bay
The Needles
Light House
Main Bench
The Nodes

RYDE
APPLEY

Sandown Bay

White Cliff Bay
Culver Cliff
Bonchurch
Ventnor
Ventnor cove
Steep Hill cove
St Lawrence
Woolverton
Old Park
Mirables
Buckaster Cove

Shanklin Chine
Dunnose
Luccomb Chine
Chine Head

Freshwater Bay

PLATE 19

SOUTHAMPTON

John Tallis

*Index-Gazetteer of the World...Illustrated with Plans of
the Principal Towns in Great Britain, America etc. Drawn and
Engraved from the Most Recent Government Surveys,
and Other Authentic Documents, c.1855*

Southampton is a town in Hampshire which stands on the River Itchin, Southampton Water and the Southwestern Railway, 12 miles from Winchester, and 79 miles from London. It ranks as a great head sea-port, commands inland navigation up the Itchin to Winchester, is a focus of railway lines for the south parts of Hampshire, and has easy railway communication with all parts of the kingdom.

Southampton fell greatly into decay after a terrible visitation of plague in 1695 and experienced increase of decay from the successful rivalry of Portsmouth. The town began to revive about the beginning of the nineteenth century, through visits of the Duke of York and through business arising from the Continental Wars. It received a powerful rise from the opening of the Southwestern Railway to it in 1840, and from the subsequent formation of docks. Commerce is much more extensive than trade. The harbour is both capacious and accessible and has excellent artificial appurtenances. A wooden landing-pier, 1,000 feet long and 36 feet wide, was constructed in 1833, at a cost of £30,000. A tidal dock of 16 acres, with 3,100 feet of quayage, and with from 18 to 21 feet of water, was completed in 1842, at a cost of £140,000. There are also a floating dock for ships, a dock for colliers and three graving docks. The vessels belonging to the port, at the beginning of 1844, were 136 small sailing vessels of aggregately 3,713 tons, 110 large sailing vessels of aggregately 15,016 tons, 14 small vessels of aggregately 404 tons and 24 large steam vessels of aggregately 7,651 tons. Ship-building, coach-building, sugar-refining, brewing and the manufacture of silks and carpets are carried on.

General markets are held on Tuesdays, Thursdays and Saturdays; a corn-market on Fridays; fairs on May 6 and 7, and on Trinity Monday and Tuesday; and a regatta in August. The population increased sixfold between 1801 and 1861, and stands at 35,305.

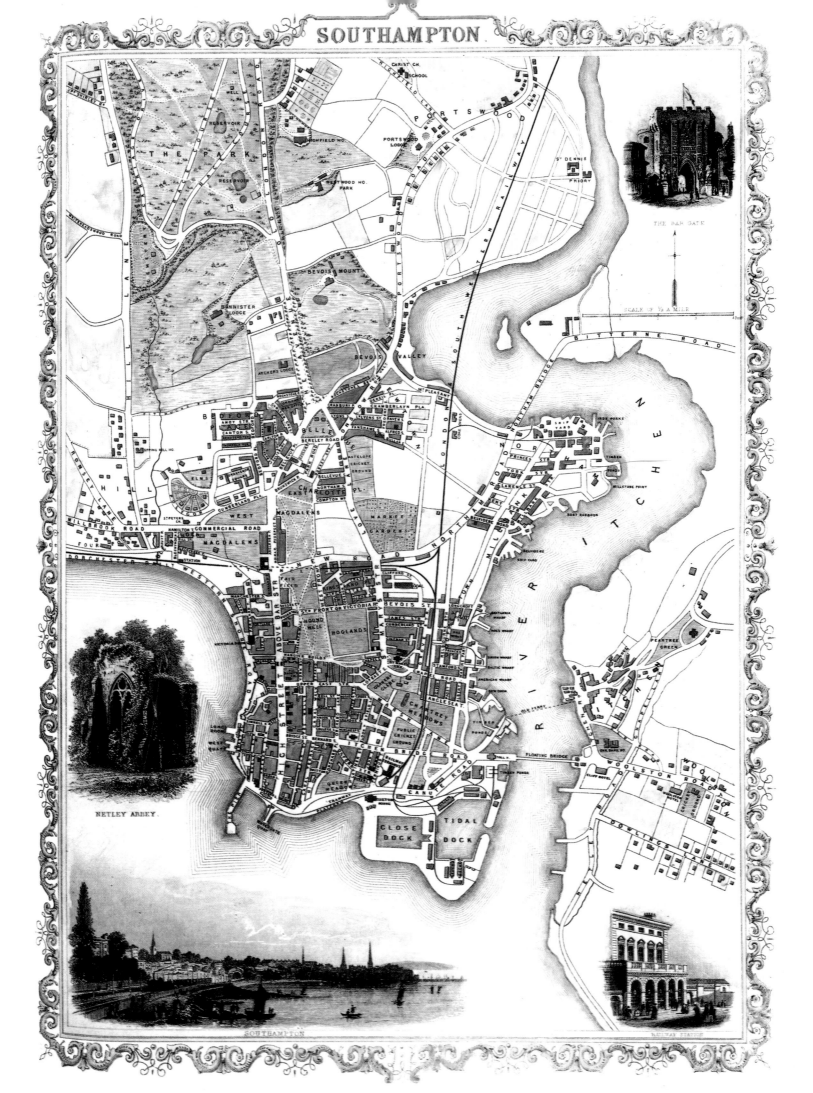

SOUTHAMPTON

THE BAR GATE

SCALE OF ½ A MILE

NETLEY ABBEY.

SOUTHAMPTON

RAILWAY STATION

LIST OF ILLUSTRATIONS

BIBLIOGRAPHY

The local descriptions accompanying the plates in this book have been compiled from the following sources:

Barclay, James, *Barclay's Complete and Universal Dictionary*, London, 1842.

Britton, John and Brayley, Edward, *The Beauties of England and Wales*, London, 1801-1818.

Gorton, John, *Topographical Dictionary of Great Britain and Ireland*, London, 1831-1833.

Lewis, Samuel, *Topographical Dictionary of England*, London, 1831.

Lewis, Samuel, *Topographical Dictionary of Ireland*, London, 1837.

Lewis, Samuel, *Topographical Dictionary of Scotland*, London, 1837.

Smith, David, *Victorian Maps of the British Isles*, London, 1985.

Tallis, John, *Tallis's Topographical Dictionary of England and Wales*, London, *c.* 1860.

Wilson, John Marius, *The Imperial Gazetteer of England and Wales*, London, 1866-1869.